Nature's Children

SHEEP

by Dan Doyle

Grolier Educational

FACTS IN BRIEF

Classification of the domestic sheep.

Class:	*Mammalia* (mammals)
Order:	*Artiodactyla* (even-toed mammals)
Family:	*Bovidae* (hollow-horned ruminants)
Sub family:	*Caprinae*
Genus:	*Ovis* (sheep)
Species:	*Ovis aries* (domestic sheep only)

World Distribution. Nearly 40 subspecies of wild sheep are found in areas from western North America to northern Africa. Domestic sheep are found in nearly every inhabitable part of the globe.

Wild Habitat. High, arid plains and hilly and mountainous regions.

Distinctive physical characteristics. Wild rams have large, spiraling horns. Ewes may or may not have horns. Some domestic sheep have horns but are better known for their white to black woolly coats. Sheep vary greatly in size, and all have split hoofs.

Habits. Sheep live in flocks and graze during daylight hours. Rams engage in head-butting spectacles during the fall.

Diet. Grass and other plants in their habitat.

Library of Congress Cataloging-in-Publication Data

Doyle, Dan. 1961-
    Sheep / Dan Doyle.
       p.   cm. — (Nature's children)
    Includes index.
    Summary: Describes the physical characteristics, behavior,
habitat, and uses of sheep, focusing on those found on a farm.
    ISBN 0-7172-9122-7 (hardbound)
    1. Sheep—Juvenile literature. [1. Sheep.] I. Title.
II. Series.
SF375.2.D69 1997
599.649—dc21

97-5972
CIP
AC

This library reinforced edition was published in 1997 exclusively by:

 Grolier Educational

Sherman Turnpike, Danbury, Connecticut 06816

Set ISBN 0-7172-7661-9
Sheep ISBN 0-7172-9122-7

Contents

Sheep are among the most useful animals ever tamed and raised by humans.

Sheep were among the first animals ever domesticated, or tamed and raised, by humans. And they are among the most important.

Sheep have clothed and fed us for centuries. In fact, some economies have been based upon sheep and sheepherding. Even today in some parts of the world, a person's wealth is measured by how many sheep he or she owns.

One of the major reasons why sheep have been so important is that their needs are quite simple. Sheep require little care, and their gentle, shy temperaments make them easy to work with.

The size and appearance of domestic sheep vary by breed. But their most obvious characteristic is the heavy growth of wool on their bodies. This wool, called fleece, can be white, brown, gray, black, or even a mix of these colors. Regardless, however, it does more than keep sheep warm. It also provides the sheep's owner with income—and the rest of us with dozens of useful products.

Where They Are Found

Sheep are not just easy to raise. They also are able to survive in many different climates and habitats.

Over thousands of years, sheep owners have bred sheep to bring out particular traits and qualities. As a result, there are sheep that live happily in the cold wet climate of Scotland and sheep that do well in the hot, dry deserts of the American Southwest.

Around the world Australia leads all countries in sheep production with about 170 million sheep. Russia is second with almost 140 million, while China follows with about 114 million.

The United States also is a big sheep-producing nation. Texas is the biggest sheep-raising state, with California, Wyoming, Montana, and South Dakota rounding out the top five. Sheep are also raised in the Midwest and the East, although not on the large scale of the sheep ranches of the West.

In countries like Australia and New Zealand, sheep are raised in herds of thousands of animals.

*Sheep like these merinos are raised
mainly for their valuable wool.*

The Useful Sheep

With the possible exception of cattle, no other domestic animal is as useful to people as sheep. Different breeds have different uses, but wool is probably the most common of all sheep products. For thousands of years, people have depended on sheep for warm, long-lasting material for clothing, blankets, felt, and other needs.

The use of sheep for meat goes back thousands of years as well. About 200 years ago, however, humans began to breed and raise sheep specifically for their meat. As a result, sheep now feed millions and millions of people each year.

There are many other uses for sheep as well. In Germany, East Fresian sheep are raised for their rich, creamy, protein-rich milk. In France, sheep produce the milk used in Roquefort cheese. And in far-off Uzbekistan karakul sheep are raised to make leather clothing.

Sheep also furnish the raw materials needed to make glue, soap, and fertilizer. Lanolin for cosmetics and ointments, tallow for candles, and the "gut" strings of tennis rackets are some of the other things that come to us from the useful sheep.

Acting Sheepish

People often associate particular animals with certain ways of behaving. There is the busy beaver, the loyal dog, the quiet mouse, and the courageous lion. If you are doing well at something, you might be said to "soar like an eagle." Or, if you've been unlucky, you might have been "skunked."

What do people think of when they think of sheep? The first words that come to mind often are timid, shy, or quiet. In fact a flock of sheep grazing in a meadow seems to be a perfect picture of peace and harmony. In the same way, lambs (young sheep) are almost always described as being gentle and loving. But, on the other hand, we think of rams (male sheep) as being strong, tough, and powerful.

These ideas might seem to contradict one another. But, as anyone who has raised or cared for sheep will tell you, sheep are all of this and more.

Sheep often bring to mind words such as timid, shy, and quiet.

Baas, Bleats, Barks, and Hisses

Lambs go "baa baa" and ewes (female sheep) go "bleat." But those aren't the only sounds made by sheep.

Both domestic and wild ewes, for example, are known to make a barking sound that is similar to a dog's bark. Ewes, however, make this sound only when they become worried or frightened.

For example, if a predator wanders near a flock of sheep, the ewes probably will see, hear, or smell this enemy first. Then they will "bark" a warning so the flock can run away by the time the predator gets close enough to attack.

An even more unusual sheep noise is the sound of old rams butting their heads against rocks. Why do they do it? Strangely, this behavior isn't caused by anger or even by fear. Instead, it is one of the ways rams mark their territory and tell other rams to stay away.

Except for this head butting, rams are basically silent. They do, however, make a strange hissing noise from their nostrils when they chase ewes during the mating season.

Sheep sometimes may make odd noises, but for the most part they are quiet animals.

This Orkney ram has a black face and horns with a great sweeping curve.

Sheepish Facts

Today there are hundreds of breeds of domestic sheep, ranging from the long-wool Leicester to the fine-wool merino. Some, like the cheviot, have white faces; others, like the Hampshire and the Oxford, have dark brown or even black faces.

In general, sheep are classified according to the type of wool they have. Fine-wool sheep like the merino have a fleece that has small fibers and many crimps (curls) per inch (2.54 centimeters). The fibers in the fleece of a long-wool sheep, on the other hand, sometimes reach a foot (30.48 centimeters) in length. Medium-wool sheep, with fleece that is somewhere in between the two extremes, are often used for their meat.

Regardless of exactly what they look like, however, all modern domestic sheep are descended from just a few ancestors. Scientists believe that sheep and goats have a common ancestor, an animal that lived in Asia and Europe about 13 million years ago.

A History Lesson

More than 9,000 years ago Stone Age farmers in the Middle East began raising the Asiatic Mouflon sheep. Soon afterward people moved into Europe with small flocks of these sheep. As the years passed, farmers slowly changed the appearance of the sheep by breeding only those with desirable qualities (like thick woolly coats and lots of meat). By 3000 BC domestic sheep looked much like they do today.

Although farmers in the Middle East and Europe had small flocks of sheep, it was the ancient Romans who were the first to raise sheep on a large scale. The Romans bred sheep carefully, raising the animals on a large scale in both Spain and Britain.

As the years passed, farmers continued to carefully select the sheep they wanted to breed. By 1400 AD the merino sheep was being used as part of a large wool industry in Spain. Herds of up to 10,000 merino sheep were kept in Spanish pastures. Sheep became so important to Spain's economy that it was illegal to send sheep out of the country alive.

An American Tail

European settlers brought the first domestic sheep to North America in the 1500s. The merino was one of the first breeds to be brought over, but others soon followed. Soon sheep were a familiar sight on the farms of New England and in the Spanish provinces of the West.

After the American Revolution sheep raising spread even more. By the time the Wild West was settled, in the 1800s, sheep found themselves homes on the large, open ranges from Montana to Texas and from Iowa to California.

By 1900 there were almost 600 million sheep on our planet, and the future of sheep ranching seemed bright. But strangely, after World War I ended in 1918, sheep production around the world fell sharply. Instead, many countries chose to focus on raising cattle.

Sheep seldom stay unwanted for long, however. Sheep raising recovered by 1945 as World War II came to an end. Today there are about 800 million domestic sheep living in nearly every part of the globe where there are people.

Bighorn sheep, one of the great wild sheep of North America, have been hunted to the brink of extinction.

Some Wild Ones

Most of the world's sheep today are domesticated, living under the supervision of humans. But there are still more than 40 different breeds of wild sheep left in the world. These creatures live in parts of Asia, North Africa, Europe, Siberia, and North America.

Most of these wild sheep, though, look more like goats than like their domestic relatives. In fact few of them even have the woolly coats that have made domestic sheep so famous—and useful.

Some of these wild breeds have a remarkable appearance. Bighorn sheep, for example, live in the mountains of western North America. Bighorn rams carry some of the largest, most impressive horns in the entire animal kingdom. Unfortunately for the bighorns, however, these horns are much sought after by collectors, who have hunted the bighorn almost to extinction.

Another impressive wild sheep is the argali, of Siberia and Mongolia. Standing 4 feet (1.2 meters) tall, these are the largest of all wild sheep. Their horns are extremely large too, growing in a giant spiral that can be more than two feet (61 centimeters) across!

Like their wild cousins, domestic sheep naturally form herds.

Lessons from the Wild

Studying the habits of wild sheep has taught people much about the behavior of sheep that are raised on ranches and farms. Wild sheep, for example, live in herds, just as their domestic cousins do. Most of these herds have fewer than 50 sheep, which is far fewer than live together on the large ranches of Australia or the North American West.

The wild herds are different in another way, too. In the wild adult rams tend to live alone or in small groups of other rams. The ewes live by themselves, too, joined only by their young male offspring. Adult males and females mix only during the mating season (called the rutting season), which takes place in the late fall. But when autumn comes, the males put on a spectacular display of head butting and other habits to attract the ewes to mate.

As spring arrives the ewes give birth, to usually no more than three lambs. As soon as the lambs are born, however, the flock moves on to higher ground, which is safer for them. Wild sheep move downhill only in winter in search of warmer weather and better grazing.

A Most Unusual Courtship

The fall rutting season is the time for one of the most dramatic of all sheep behaviors, one that lets people know that there is a good reason why male sheep are called rams. During this period, rams are known for making head-on charges at one another, banging their heads and horns together as forcefully as possible.

The rams do this to show each other just who is strongest and most powerful. But this isn't just for the benefit of other rams. It is done to attract the watching ewes.

The charge begins with both animals backing up and then sprinting forward head on. Just before they hit, they rise up on their back legs and drop forward with all their weight, crashing into each other's horns. The sound of the blows often can be heard over a mile (1.6 kilometers) away!

Surprisingly, the rams are rarely hurt by all of this. They are protected by extremely strong skulls and by horns that are always growing. The fights are also governed by a remarkable code of honor. Only rams with equal-sized horns, for example, ever fight each other. And neither animal charges until both are ready.

A ram's horns get a lot of use during mating season.

Sheep or Goat?

Sheep and goats, of course, are close cousins, both being descended from the same prehistoric ancestor. In fact, these two creatures often look so much alike that wild sheep are often confused with goats. There are, however, some important differences in the appearance and habitats of the two animals.

Goats, for example, are thinner than sheep, with thick, upturned tails. Male goats, called billy goats, have beards. Beyond this, wild sheep usually live in hilly regions, while the natural habitat of wild goats is higher up in the mountain ranges.

Sheep and goats actually can get along well with each other, and many farms and ranches raise both kinds of animals in the same area. But goats actually are a bit hardier than sheep. For the most part, sheep graze on grass. Goats, on the other hand, have adapted to extremely poor conditions. They often can be seen browsing around the edges of a pasture eating the thorny scrubs and bushes.

Although they often look very much like sheep, goats like these have slimmer bodies.

Domestic Sheep Breeds

The Spanish merino was the first important domestic sheep of modern times. It was so important, in fact, that nearly all of today's domestic sheep are related to it in one way or another.

Despite this connection, breeds of sheep can be amazingly different from one another. There are large breeds and small breeds, sheep with no horns and sheep with one, two, or even four horns.

There even are sheep—called hairy sheep—that do not have any wool at all. These animals, which are raised for milk and meat, actually shed their hair each spring.

Woolly sheep are the most common of all today. They also are the most different from their ancestors. Over time they have been bred to have a woolly fleece instead of the coarse hair that covered their wild ancestors.

Woolly sheep are sheared once a year, usually in the late spring. An official classification system divides their fleece—and sheep—into five groups. Depending on the texture and quality of their wool, there is fine wool, long wool, crossbred wool, medium wool, and coarse wool. As you might expect, fine-wool brings the best price, and the fine wool breeds are the most valuable.

Some breeds, like this four-horned Manx Loghtan ram from England, are rare today.

Why the Merino Is So Famous

There is no doubt that the merino is the most famous of all domestic sheep breeds. What made the merino so important?

Physically, purebred merinos are fairly small, with large rams weighing only about 200 pounds (90 kilograms). They have white faces and a whitish-colored fleece.

Merino rams usually have big horns. Ewes, which generally weigh around 150 pounds (67.5 kilograms), have no horns. There also is a merino variety that is "polled," which means that it has no horns at all; it is less important than the standard breed, however.

What really has separated the merino from other sheep, however, is its fleece. A full-grown merino ewe can produce more than 10 pounds (4.5 kilograms) of wool each year, while a merino ram yields a whopping 20 pounds (9 kilograms). With so much wool at stake, no wonder people were anxious to breed their sheep with the heavy-coated merino!

The merino, which originally came from Spain, is perhaps the world's most famous sheep.

Many new breeds of sheep were created by crossbreeding individual sheep with valuable merinos, like these rams.

Crossbreeding

As wonderful as the merino sheep is, it did not take long before shepherds and farmers tried to improve the breed. They did this by breeding their merinos with other sheep. Known as crossbreeding, this led to many new kinds of domestic sheep. As the practice caught on, breeders around the world created dozens of breeds, almost all of which were based on the Spanish merino and its descendant, the French Rambouillet.

The principles of crossbreeding are simple. As merino sheep were imported into other countries, shepherds and farmers made sure that only the best sheep were allowed to be bred together. In an area that valued meat, local shepherds would breed sheep that had the most and the best meat. If a particular type of wool was needed, the shepherds and farmers developed sheep with precisely that kind of coat.

As a result of this crossbreeding we now have all types of sheep for all types of purposes. There even are dual purpose sheep that provide both wool and meat. As you might expect, these are quickly becoming the most popular of all domestic sheep.

West of the Mississippi River, large herds of sheep graze on range land.

At Home on the Range

In North America most domestic sheep roam ranges west of the Mississippi River. These sheep spend just about all of their time outdoors, eating grass and sticking together in herds of upwards of 2,000 sheep.

Range sheep are moved around fairly often in order to get them the best grass and weather. This usually is done by the ranchers and their sheepdogs, which bark, chase, and herd the sheep from one area to another.

Most American ranchers prefer woolly sheep because the warm coats and rugged bodies of these animals make them well suited to the cold winters on the range. Also, woolly sheep generally do not need much water. This is a useful characteristic in those parts of the West in which water can be scarce.

East of the Mississippi River it is more common for sheep to be raised on farms. Here flocks of fewer than 300 sheep live in barns or sheds and graze in fenced-in pastures.

Regardless of whether they are raised on the range or in pastures, sheep cling together. Staying close to one another in their flocks, they can be warned of any approaching predator and can flee at the slightest sign of danger.

Something to Chew On

Did you ever notice how sheep always seem to be chewing something? What they are chewing is their cud, and it is one of the many interesting things about sheep. Here's how it works.

A sheep eats grass and swallows it. The grass is then stored in one of four compartments in the sheep's stomach. There the swallowed grass gets soft and forms small lumps called cud.

When a sheep rests, its stomach muscles send the cud back up into its mouth. There the cud is chewed once again before being swallowed once and for all.

Eating this way helps sheep get the most nutrition from their food. As a result even range-raised sheep — who often have to work very hard to find grass to eat—can survive quite well. Given extra nutrients (as Eastern, farm-raised sheep often are) sheep can grow fatter and provide even more wool.

Enemies

Like most domestic animals, sheep must be protected from enemies that can harm their health or take their lives. For sheep some of these enemies are extremely small but just as deadly as a four-legged predator.

Sheep, for example, often have problems with parasites. Tiny worms can attach themselves to a sheep's stomach lining and intestines. These creatures then feed on the animal's blood and fluids. Infected sheep become so weak that sometimes they cannot reproduce or even survive. If the parasites are not eliminated, whole flocks of sheep can be destroyed.

Other parasites attack the sheep externally. Flies, ticks, mites, and worms attach themselves to a sheep's fleece, skin, or nostrils or even to cuts on its body. These too can cause major problems.

Even today predators are one of the biggest threats to sheep. Coyotes will attack and eat lambs, while wolves and mountain lions can easily kill an adult sheep. But the biggest nuisance is pet dogs, which often hurt or kill sheep. Fortunately sheepdogs are able to chase off most of these enemies, even ferocious mountain lions.

One of the most important jobs for a shepherd is to protect the baby lambs.

A Vanishing Way of Life

The life of a shepherd is based on age-old ways that are slowly vanishing. In many parts of the world huge companies that specialize in large-scale sheep raising are taking over the industry. Elsewhere cities and towns have sprawled out onto the countryside, making pasture land too expensive to use for raising sheep. For these reasons the old-fashioned shepherd is passing into history, although a few can still be found today.

A shepherd's days are spent in the outdoors with animals. If they live in an area in which grass is plentiful, the shepherds can keep their flocks in the same area all year long. Otherwise, the shepherds and flocks go up into the mountains each spring. There they look for good grasslands and stay for as long as six months at a time.

The shepherd's job is simple: to protect the flocks from predators and to keep the sheep healthy. It is a quiet life, with the shepherd, sheepdogs, and sheep all sleeping under the stars at night and living with whatever weather comes their way. But shepherds say this life gives them a feeling of peace, freedom, and accomplishment, something that is hard to find on a large-scale sheep-raising operation.

Welsh Corgis are among the best sheepdogs in the world.

The Loyal Sheepdog

For hundreds of years shepherds have relied on one tool to help them—their faithful sheepdogs. Fast on their feet and quick of mind, these dogs are able to keep a herd of sheep together all on their own. And, just as important, these courageous dogs will risk their lives to protect flocks from coyotes, wolves, mountain lions, and even other dogs.

Always on duty, sheepdogs watch their flocks during the day. They round up strays that wander from the flock and drive the flock from one grazing area to another. During the day the dogs sometimes will doze off for a nap, knowing that the shepherd is awake to watch over the flock. Somehow, though, the dogs always wake when it is time to find a stray or scare off an enemy of one kind or another.

Most dangers to the flock come at night or in the early morning hours. And that is when a sheepdog is most alert. Warned by its bark, the sheep wake and come flocking to their four-legged guardian, the ever-watchful sheepdog.

Shearing is a major activity on large sheep ranches, like this one in Montana.

Time for a Trim

Wild sheep have a hairy coat that stays with them all year long. In the winter, a woolly fleece grows in between these hairs. This undercoat keeps them warm during the cold months and is shed when spring arrives.

Through careful breeding these hairs have disappeared from domestic sheep. Instead, they have only their woolly fleece. Even the woolliest breeds of domestic sheep rarely shed. Rather, they are sheared, or clipped, once a year.

Shearing usually is done in the spring, when temperatures are rising and the heavy wool coat would be too hot and uncomfortable for the sheep anyway. Shearing also helps remove ticks, lice, mites, and dirt, which keeps the sheep cleaner and healthier.

Shearing can be done with either manual, hand-operated scissors or with electric shears. On small farms it is usually done by the shepherd. But, on large-scale ranches, shearing may be done by specialists who travel from place to place during the shearing season.

In the hands of an expert shearer, the sheep's wool comes off quickly and in one piece. In minutes the unharmed sheep is back grazing in the pasture or on the range.

Measuring Wool

Shearing, of course, is not the end of the sheep's fleece. Afterward the wool is rolled, tied, and sent to market. There it is washed. It also is given a value that is based on the weight of the clean wool, the breed of the sheep, and the quality of the wool produced by a particular sheep.

There are three ways to classify the quality of a sheep's wool. The "spinning count" is the oldest method, and it is based on how many yards of yarn are produced by one pound of clean wool. The spinning count is expressed in even numbers, and the highest rating usually is around 80.

Another system, the "blood system," was originally used to describe what fraction of a sheep's blood, or ancestry, came from the merino sheep. No one today really keeps track of how much merino ancestry is in each sheep. But the system is still used sometimes to describe the quality of a breed's wool.

The "micron system" is the most modern and the most scientific. It also is the most accurate way to measure wool quality because, in the micron system, people actually measure the size of the wool fiber.

Once the fleece is off the sheep, it can be rolled, tied, and sent to market.

Breeding

As you might imagine, breeding is extremely important for people raising sheep. Not only does breeding make sure that there are always new lambs for wool or meat, it also helps farmers and shepherds improve their sheep.

Each year the ewes in a flock go into heat, which is the time during which they can become pregnant. This can happen as early as August or as late as December depending on the breed of the sheep and where they are living.

This is the rutting, or mating, season, and it goes on for several months. During this time the rams put on their courtship displays, trying to scare off other rams and to attract ewes.

Since the farmers want only certain sheep to breed, at this point they carefully separate the ewes from the rams. They also separate brothers and sisters and mothers and fathers. Inbreeding (allowing closely related sheep to breed with one another) can lead to problems in the lambs.

Finally, the females are divided into groups of about 30 ewes each. Then one ram is let loose with each group. Soon, ewes will start becoming pregnant and new lambs will be born.

It takes almost a year before a lamb is ready to move off and live on its own, away from its mother.

Pregnancy and Birth

The gestation period, or pregnancy, of female sheep usually lasts for about 145 days. During this time they need shelter, extra food and water, and plenty of exercise. If they get it, there is every chance that their lambs will be healthy, strong additions to the flock.

Spring is usually the birthing, or lambing, time for a ewe. When she is ready to give birth, a ewe often becomes restless. She even starts to ignore her food. Then, when the actual time comes, she is likely to wander off by herself. Ewes frequently give birth in a barn or in a private area of the range or pasture.

Once a lamb is born, the ewe cleans it thoroughly. Few animal mothers pay as much attention to their young as a ewe. For three to five months the mother feeds the lamb her milk. Then slowly the lambs are weaned, leaving behind their mother's milk and living on a diet of grass and other grains.

After a year, the mother pushes away her lamb, sending it off on its own. This makes room for new lambs to be born. And it gives the lamb time to grow and become an adult, ready to breed more sheep at the beginning of the next rutting season.

Words to Know

Bighorn sheep   A wild sheep of North America noted for its large horns.

Bleat   The name given to the "baaaa" sound lambs and ewes make.

Crossbreeding   The coupling of two different species to form a third species.

Cud   A clump of grass that is swallowed, regurgitated, chewed, and swallowed again.

Ewe   A female sheep.

Fleece   Another name for wool.

Flock   A group of sheep.

Heat   The time during which a ewe can become pregnant.

Polled   A variety of sheep, goat, or cattle that is without horns.

Predator   A creature that lives by killing and eating others.

Ram   A male sheep.

Range   The fenceless grasslands formerly found in the western states.

Ruminant   A cud-chewing animal that is cloven-hoofed.

Rutting season   A period in the fall when sheep mate.

Shear   To cut wool from a sheep.

INDEX

Cover Photo: Norvia Behling (Behling & Johnson Photography)
Photo Credits: Norvia Behling (Behling & Johnson Photography), pages 11, 36, 38, 45; Sharon Cummings (Dembinsky Photo Associates), page 25; Michael Francis (The Wildlife Collection), pages 32, 40; John Giustina (The Wildlife Collection), page 4; Lynn M. Stone, pages 8, 14, 18, 20, 22, 26, 28, 30, 42; SuperStock, Inc., pages 7, 13.